U.S. WARS

WORLD WAR II IN EUROPE

A MyReportLinks.com Book

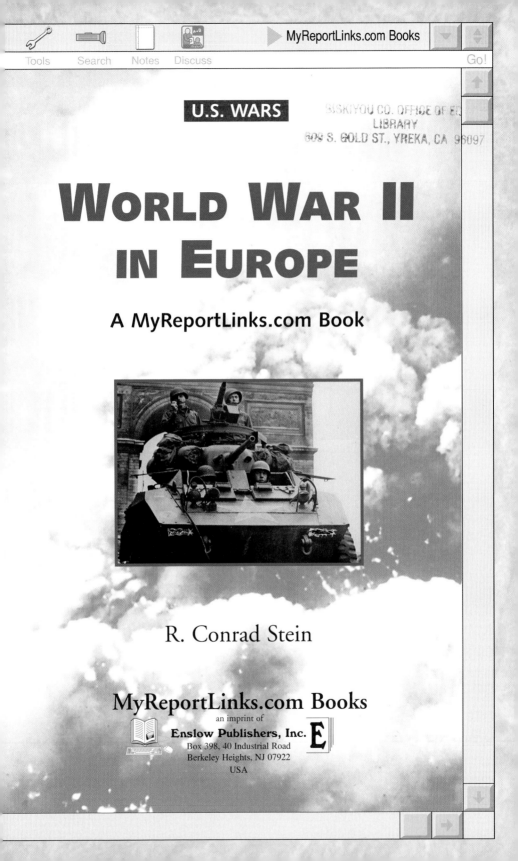

R. Conrad Stein

MyReportLinks.com Books
an imprint of
Enslow Publishers, Inc. E
Box 398, 40 Industrial Road
Berkeley Heights, NJ 07922
USA

MyReportLinks.com Books, an imprint of Enslow Publishers, Inc. MyReportLinks is a trademark of Enslow Publishers, Inc.

Library of Congress Cataloging-in-Publication Data

Stein, R. Conrad.
　　World War II in Europe / R. Conrad Stein.
　　　　p. cm. — (U.S. Wars)
　　Includes bibliographical references and index.
　　Summary: Examines the origins of World War II in Europe and discusses battles, military tactics, weaponry, new methods of destruction, and America's involvement in the war. Includes Internet links to Web sites, source documents, and photographs related to the war.
　　ISBN 0-7660-5094-7
　　1. World War, 1939–1945—Europe—Juvenile literature. [1. World War, 1939–1945—Europe.] I. Title. II. Title: World War Two in Europe. III. Title: World War 2 in Europe. IV. Series.
D743.7 .S748 2002
940.54—dc21

　　　　　　　　　　　　　　　　　　2001008192

Printed in the United States of America

10 9 8 7 6 5 4 3 2 1

To Our Readers:
Through the purchase of this book, you and your library gain access to the Report Links that specifically back up this book.

The Publisher will provide access to the Report Links that back up this book and will keep these Report Links up to date on **www.myreportlinks.com** for three years from the book's first publication date.

We have done our best to make sure all Internet addresses in this book were active and appropriate when we went to press. However, the author and the Publisher have no control over, and assume no liability for, the material available on those Internet sites or on other Web sites they may link to.

The usage of the MyReportLinks.com Books Web site is subject to the terms and conditions stated on the Usage Policy Statement on **www.myreportlinks.com**.

In the future, a password may be required to access the Report Links that back up this book. The password is found on the bottom of page 4 of this book.

Any comments or suggestions can be sent by e-mail to comments@myreportlinks.com or to the address on the back cover.

Photo Credits: © Corel Corporation, pp. 1 (background), 3; America's Story from America's Library/Library of Congress, pp. 19, 21, 23, 30, 41; Encarta Encyclopedia, pp. 11, 17, 28, 33, 35; Encyclopedia Britannica Online, p. 38; Grolier Encyclopedia, p. 44; MyReportLinks.com Books, p. 4; Thinkquest Library, pp. 15, 25; Webpub at Allegheny College, pp. 31, 43.

Cover Photo: National Archives

Cover Description: American troops in tank passing the Arc de Triomphe after the liberation of Paris, August 1944.

Contents

MyReportLinks.com Books
Great Books, Great Links, Great for Research!

MyReportLinks.com Books present the information you need to learn about your report subject. In addition, they show you where to go on the Internet for more information. The pre-evaluated Report Links that back up this book are kept up to date on **www.myreportlinks.com**. With the purchase of a MyReportLinks.com Books title, you and your library gain access to the Report Links that specifically back up that book. The Report Links save hours of research time and link to dozens—even hundreds—of Web sites, source documents, and photos related to your report topic.

Please see "To Our Readers" on the Copyright page for important information about this book, the MyReportLinks.com Books Web site, and the Report Links that back up this book.

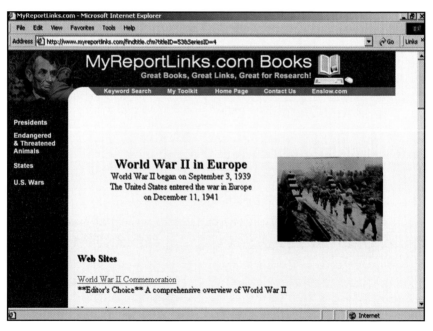

Access:

The Publisher will provide access to the Report Links that back up this book and will try to keep these Report Links up to date on our Web site for three years from the book's first publication date. Please enter **UWE2739** if asked for a password.

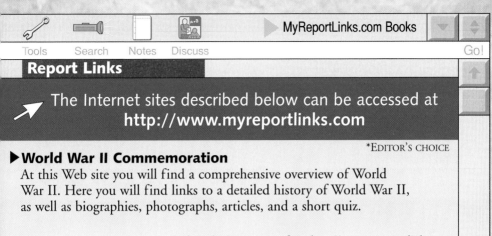
*EDITOR'S CHOICE

▶ World War II Commemoration

At this Web site you will find a comprehensive overview of World
War II. Here you will find links to a detailed history of World War II,
as well as biographies, photographs, articles, and a short quiz.

Link to this Internet site from http://www.myreportlinks.com

*EDITOR'S CHOICE

▶ Normandy 1944

Britannica Online's site chronicles the buildup, invasion, and aftermath
of the invasion of Normandy in 1944, otherwise known as D-Day. It
also includes thorough descriptions of the events leading up to the
invasion as well as photographs of the battle itself.

Link to this Internet site from http://www.myreportlinks.com

*EDITOR'S CHOICE

▶ Anne Frank Online

This site provides a wealth of information on the life of Anne Frank.
In addition to her famous diary, the site addresses the historic context
that produced it.

Link to this Internet site from http://www.myreportlinks.com

*EDITOR'S CHOICE

▶ Maps of the World War II European Theater

This site is a collection of eighty-three full-color maps of military
campaigns in Europe during the war. These detailed maps can serve as
a great companion to other, more text-heavy World War II sites.

Link to this Internet site from http://www.myreportlinks.com

*EDITOR'S CHOICE

▶ The Holocaust: A Tragic Legacy

Thinkquest's site teaches the Holocaust through various interactive
learning tools. Among them are an interactive time line, a virtual tour
of a concentration camp, and quizzes to test your knowledge of
the Holocaust.

Link to this Internet site from http://www.myreportlinks.com

*EDITOR'S CHOICE

▶ American Masters: World War II

This PBS Web site highlights well-known intellectuals, whose lives were
threatened during World War II. Here you will find the biographies of
Albert Einstein, Arthur Rubinstein, Man Ray, and other intellectuals
who immigrated to the United States during the war.

Link to this Internet site from http://www.myreportlinks.com

Report Links

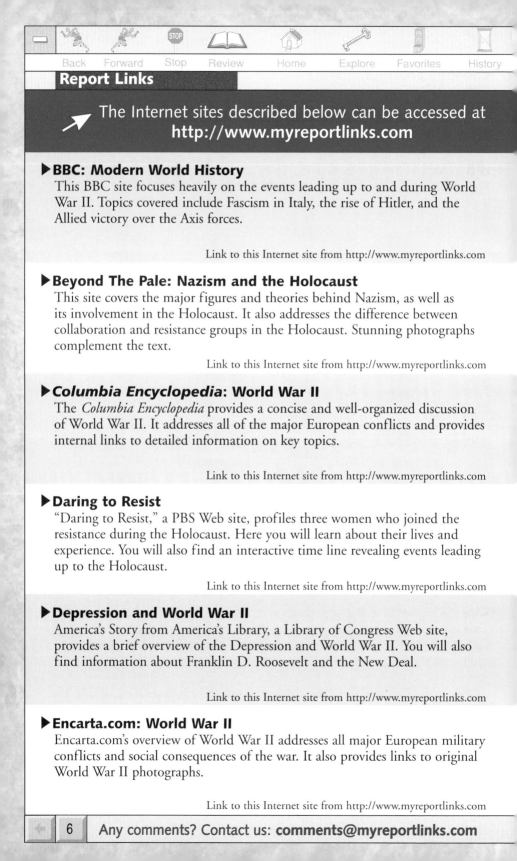

The Internet sites described below can be accessed at
http://www.myreportlinks.com

▶**BBC: Modern World History**
This BBC site focuses heavily on the events leading up to and during World
War II. Topics covered include Fascism in Italy, the rise of Hitler, and the
Allied victory over the Axis forces.

Link to this Internet site from http://www.myreportlinks.com

▶**Beyond The Pale: Nazism and the Holocaust**
This site covers the major figures and theories behind Nazism, as well as
its involvement in the Holocaust. It also addresses the difference between
collaboration and resistance groups in the Holocaust. Stunning photographs
complement the text.

Link to this Internet site from http://www.myreportlinks.com

▶*Columbia Encyclopedia*: **World War II**
The *Columbia Encyclopedia* provides a concise and well-organized discussion
of World War II. It addresses all of the major European conflicts and provides
internal links to detailed information on key topics.

Link to this Internet site from http://www.myreportlinks.com

▶**Daring to Resist**
"Daring to Resist," a PBS Web site, profiles three women who joined the
resistance during the Holocaust. Here you will learn about their lives and
experience. You will also find an interactive time line revealing events leading
up to the Holocaust.

Link to this Internet site from http://www.myreportlinks.com

▶**Depression and World War II**
America's Story from America's Library, a Library of Congress Web site,
provides a brief overview of the Depression and World War II. You will also
find information about Franklin D. Roosevelt and the New Deal.

Link to this Internet site from http://www.myreportlinks.com

▶**Encarta.com: World War II**
Encarta.com's overview of World War II addresses all major European military
conflicts and social consequences of the war. It also provides links to original
World War II photographs.

Link to this Internet site from http://www.myreportlinks.com

Report Links

The Internet sites described below can be accessed at
http://www.myreportlinks.com

▶ **Hitler and World War Two**
This lecture centers on Adolf Hitler and his role in World War II.
It contains original photographs and links to further reading
on key topics.

Link to this Internet site from http://www.myreportlinks.com

▶ **The Hitler Youth**
This site tells the story of Hitler's project to indoctrinate Germany's
youth population with Nazi ideology.

Link to this Internet site from http://www.myreportlinks.com

▶ **Joseph Stalin Wrote a Memo: August 13, 1942**
America's Story from America's Library, provides a brief overview of the
alliance between the United States, Great Britain, and the Soviet Union
during World War II. You will also read about the D-Day invasion.

Link to this Internet site from http://www.myreportlinks.com

▶ **Lest We Forget: World War II**
This ever-expanding site features a section dedicated to the European
theater of operations. It contains many photographs from the war, as
well as essays and commentaries on topics not typically covered.

Link to this Internet site from http://www.myreportlinks.com

▶ **Maps of World War II**
This site traces the history of World War II through maps of key battles
and military campaigns. It contains maps for all the major European
military campaigns. The maps focus on the general direction of troop
movements within the central areas of conflict.

Link to this Internet site from http://www.myreportlinks.com

▶ **Newshour Transcript: Citizen Soldiers**
In this interview transcript, historian Stephen Ambrose discusses major
events in Europe between D-Day and the end of World War II.

Link to this Internet site from http://www.myreportlinks.com

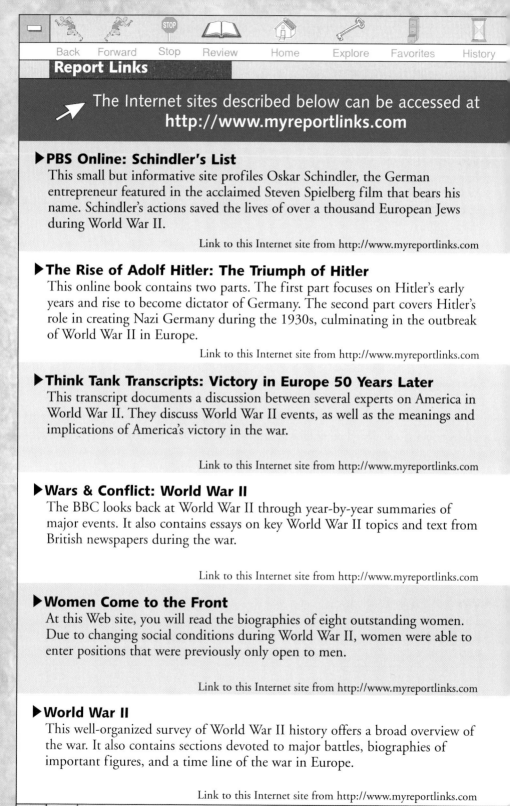

The Internet sites described below can be accessed at
http://www.myreportlinks.com

▶**PBS Online: Schindler's List**
This small but informative site profiles Oskar Schindler, the German
entrepreneur featured in the acclaimed Steven Spielberg film that bears his
name. Schindler's actions saved the lives of over a thousand European Jews
during World War II.

Link to this Internet site from http://www.myreportlinks.com

▶**The Rise of Adolf Hitler: The Triumph of Hitler**
This online book contains two parts. The first part focuses on Hitler's early
years and rise to become dictator of Germany. The second part covers Hitler's
role in creating Nazi Germany during the 1930s, culminating in the outbreak
of World War II in Europe.

Link to this Internet site from http://www.myreportlinks.com

▶**Think Tank Transcripts: Victory in Europe 50 Years Later**
This transcript documents a discussion between several experts on America in
World War II. They discuss World War II events, as well as the meanings and
implications of America's victory in the war.

Link to this Internet site from http://www.myreportlinks.com

▶**Wars & Conflict: World War II**
The BBC looks back at World War II through year-by-year summaries of
major events. It also contains essays on key World War II topics and text from
British newspapers during the war.

Link to this Internet site from http://www.myreportlinks.com

▶**Women Come to the Front**
At this Web site, you will read the biographies of eight outstanding women.
Due to changing social conditions during World War II, women were able to
enter positions that were previously only open to men.

Link to this Internet site from http://www.myreportlinks.com

▶**World War II**
This well-organized survey of World War II history offers a broad overview of
the war. It also contains sections devoted to major battles, biographies of
important figures, and a time line of the war in Europe.

Link to this Internet site from http://www.myreportlinks.com

Report Links

The Internet sites described below can be accessed at
http://www.myreportlinks.com

▶World War II

Infoplease.com's online encyclopedia provides a concise overview of
World War II. Major European conflicts and events are addressed and
internal links offer more detailed information on important topics.

Link to this Internet site from http://www.myreportlinks.com

▶World War II Collection

This site focuses primarily on World War II in northern Europe. It
contains sections on battles, important war figures, and full-color scans
of German and American war posters.

Link to this Internet site from http://www.myreportlinks.com

▶World War Two In Europe

This time line covers both the events leading up to and during World
War II in Europe. It contains links to captioned photographs of
important people, places, and events during the war.

Link to this Internet site from http://www.myreportlinks.com

▶World War II Exhibit: A People at War

This site provides an in-depth overview of World War II. It includes
information on the war in Europe and the Pacific War, as well as the
role women played during the war. Contains photographs of
prominent figures, citizens, and weapons.

Link to this Internet site from http://www.myreportlinks.com

▶World War II Unversed

This site provides a brief chronological overview of World War II.
It is concise, but provides links to more detailed discussions of
important events.

Link to this Internet site from http://www.myreportlinks.com

▶The World At War

This site contains a military history of World War II. All military
theaters are covered, but the site covers all the major battles and
conflicts within Europe.

Link to this Internet site from http://www.myreportlinks.com

European War Facts

Allies: United States; Great Britain; France; the Soviet Union; China; Australia; Canada; Italy (after Sept. 8, 1943); and others.

Axis: Germany; Japan; Italy (before Sept. 8, 1943); and others.

Casualties*	Killed	Wounded
United States	291,557	670,846
Soviet Union	6,115,000	14,012,000
Great Britain	357,116	369,267
France	201,568	400,000
Germany	3,250,000	7,250,000
Italy	149,496	66,716
Japan	1,270,000	140,000

*Casualty totals reflect all military losses, including battles fought in Europe, Africa, and Asia.

1939—*Sept. 1:* The German army invades Poland.

—*Sept. 3:* Britain and France declare war on Germany.

1941—*Dec. 11:* Germany and Italy declare war on the United States.

1942—*Nov. 8:* United States forces land in North Africa.

—*Nov. 19:* The Russian army launches a massive counterattack against the Germans.

1943—*Feb. 2:* A huge German army surrenders to the Russians at Stalingrad.

—*Aug. 17:* Sicily falls to the Allies.

—*Sept. 3:* The Allies land in Italy; a new Italian government surrenders to the United States and Great Britain.

1944—*June 6:* D-Day; Allied armies land in France.

—*Aug. 25:* Paris is liberated.

—*Dec. 6:* The Germans counterattack American lines and begin the Battle of the Bulge.

1945—*April 25:* Russian and American infantry units meet at Torgau in southern Germany.

—*April 30:* Hitler commits suicide in his Berlin bunker.

—*May 7:* Germany surrenders to the Allies.

The Battle of the Bulge

A light snow fell on the Ardennes Forest in the region of Belgium and Luxembourg. This area was Germany's back door. Allied armies were poised to break through that door and rush into the enemy homeland—Germany. However, in mid-December 1944, the front had been strangely silent for several days. Soldiers marveled at the snow that decorated the pine trees.

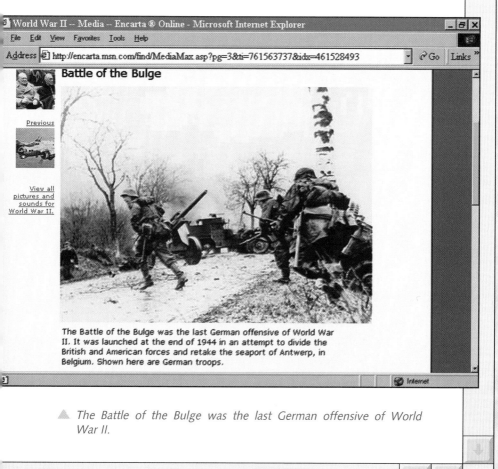

World War II -- Media -- Encarta ® Online - Microsoft Internet Explorer

File   Edit   View   Favorites   Tools   Help

Address http://encarta.msn.com/find/MediaMax.asp?pg=3&ti=761563737&idx=461528493   Go   Links

Battle of the Bulge

Previous

View all pictures and sounds for World War II.

The Battle of the Bulge was the last German offensive of World War II. It was launched at the end of 1944 in an attempt to divide the British and American forces and retake the seaport of Antwerp, in Belgium. Shown here are German troops.

▲ The Battle of the Bulge was the last German offensive of World War II.

Then a firestorm of German artillery brought horror to the lovely forest scene. From out of the woodland roads rumbled German tanks. German infantry—an incredible 300,000 troops—supported the armored vehicles. Allied officers were shocked. They thought it was impossible for the Germans to assemble such a huge army in this late stage of the war. This attack had been secretly planned for weeks. Adolf Hitler did much of the planning himself.

The German army broke through along the 60-mile-long Ardennes front. In American headquarters, a black bulge appeared on maps showing the battle lines. A newspaper writer dubbed the unexpected German offensive the Battle of the Bulge. For the first four days, American troops fell back in panic. Cooks, clerks, and members of the military band were given rifles and rushed to the front. Gradually American troops stopped the German advance. General Anthony McAuliffe became famous when he replied, "Nuts!" to a German demand for surrender.

Hitler hoped his forces would advance as far as the port city of Antwerp and split the Allied army in two. Instead, by mid-January 1945, the Germans had lost all the ground they gained in their initial assault. As one historian noted, "Showing a desperate courage that surprised the Germans, the American infantry and tankers fought back with a ferocity fueled by true tales of SS atrocities and stark anger."[1] The offensive action cost the Germans 100,000 casualties and resulted in 110,000 men taken prisoner. The Battle of the Bulge was the largest battle fought by American soldiers in World War II.

The World Goes to War

World War II was the greatest tragedy in the human experience. From the fall of 1939 through the middle of 1945, more than 55 million people died as a direct result of this worldwide clash of arms. A greater number of civilians than soldiers were killed. More than any other single event, World War II shaped life in the twentieth century.

The United States entered the war late in 1941 and was forced to fight on both sides of the globe—in the Pacific and in Europe. In the Pacific, the war was against the Japanese. This book will concentrate on United States involvement in the European war, which included fighting in North Africa.

Historians generally agree that World War II in Europe was an outgrowth of World War I, fought between 1914 and 1918. World War I killed millions and devastated the European spirit. New weapons such as machine guns and fast-firing artillery turned battle lines into nightmarish killing fields. Soldiers charged out of trenches and died on ground turned red with blood. Some young men marched into World War I dreaming of heroic deeds and knightly glory. In muddy trenches the men found only terror, suffering, and death.

Germany was the principal loser in World War I. Under a harsh settlement called the Treaty of Versailles, Germany was forced to give up territory and to pay reparations to the victors. Cash reparations sparked runaway inflation in Germany. The price of a loaf of bread jumped

from one mark to 1 million marks. Unemployment soared. Masses of Germans went hungry. Into this chaos stepped a new German leader.

▶ A Failed Artist

Adolf Hitler was born in Austria on April 20, 1889. As a young man he traveled to Vienna, where he hoped to become an artist. Professors at a prestigious Vienna art school studied Hitler's drawings, determined he lacked talent, and rejected his application for admission. Bitterly disappointed, young Hitler did odd jobs in the city. Often he carried suitcases at the train station for tips amounting to a penny or two.

When World War I broke out, Hitler enlisted in the German infantry and served with honor. In 1919, he joined the German Worker's Party, one of many political splinter groups developing at the time. It was later renamed the Nazi Party. A fiery speaker, he quickly rose to be the party's chief. In a 1932 election, the Nazi Party won close to 40 percent of the nation's vote, and Hitler was named chancellor—the leader of Germany. Around the country people began calling him *Der Führer* (*fyur-er*), which means leader.

As chancellor, Hitler eased unemployment through government projects such as a highway construction program. Ominously he rebuilt the military, despite clauses in the Versailles Treaty that forbade Germany from rearming the army, navy, or air force. He also preached hatred. In 1933, German Jews numbered less than 1 percent of the country's population. Yet the Jews, Hitler claimed, were the root cause of Germany's economic ills. He once said, "Jewish parasites plundered the nation without pity."[1] This hatred of Jews is called *anti-Semitism*.

The Road to War

The 1930s were troublesome years in Europe. A worldwide economic depression closed industries and put millions of people out of work. Dictators such as Benito Mussolini in Italy and Joseph Stalin in the Soviet Union tightened their grip over their people. In Germany, Adolf Hitler had gained absolute power over the nation.

Hitler dreamed of expanding his nation's territory and building a glorious German empire that would last a thousand years. Step-by-step, he moved against his neighbors. In March 1936, he sent troops into the

Nazis destroyed and burned Jewish businesses on Kristallnacht, or Night of the Broken Glass. Many historians believe this event, which occurred on November 9, 1938, signifies the onset of the Holocaust.

Rhineland, a territory on the border of France and Germany. Seeking to build a "greater Germany," Hitler annexed Austria in 1938. When Hitler threatened Czechoslovakia, their allies, the French and the British, stood ready to fight. Then, England and France caved in to Hitler's demands and allowed the Germans to occupy the Sudetenland, a large territory in Czechoslovakia. Next, Germany signed a secret nonaggression treaty with Joseph Stalin, the leader of the Communist Soviet Union. The treaty stipulated that the Soviet Union would stay neutral if Germany went to war.

On September 1, 1939, Hitler sent his armies storming into Poland, Germany's neighbor to the east. Poland was aligned with Great Britain and France. Hitler gambled that the French and the British would refuse to fight. This time, however, Hitler lost his bet. France and Britain declared war on Germany, and World War II in Europe officially began.

In a speech delivered in September 1939, Hitler said, "I am from now on just the first soldier of the German Reich [government]. I have once more put on that coat [army uniform] that was most sacred and dear to me. I will not take it off again until victory is secured . . ."[2]

▶ Lightning War

In the opening months of the war, the German army electrified the world. Led by tanks and riding trucks, soldiers raced into Poland. These mighty armored columns were protected by waves of screaming dive-bomber aircraft. Gone were the notions that this new war would be a repeat of the slow-moving trench fighting seen in World War I. This was called *blitzkrieg* (lightning war). It featured onrushes of German tanks, which penetrated behind the enemy's lines and shattered the foe's will to resist. Although its armies fought valiantly, Poland was crushed in just twenty days.

Germany then turned north and conquered Denmark and Norway. On May 10, 1940, German tanks swept through Belgium, Luxembourg, and the Netherlands. Those countries fell in a matter of days, allowing armored columns to rumble into France. Weeks later, German tanks surrounded 336,000 British and French troops at the port city of Dunkerque (Dunkirk in English). Most of the soldiers trapped at Dunkirk were saved through heroic efforts of the British air force and navy. Italy, Germany's

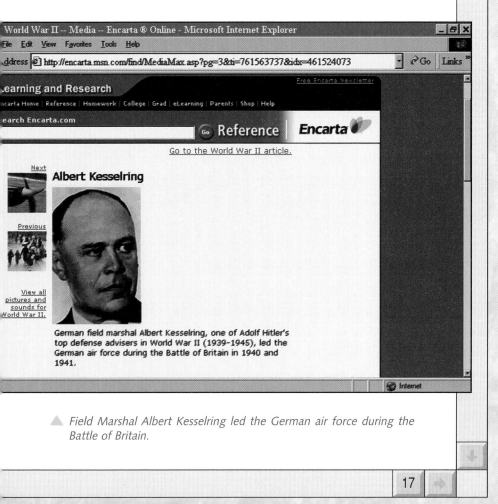

World War II -- Media -- Encarta ® Online - Microsoft Internet Explorer

File Edit View Favorites Tools Help

Address http://encarta.msn.com/find/MediaMax.asp?pg=3&ti=761563737&idx=461524073   Go   Links

Free Encarta Newsletter

Learning and Research

Encarta Home | Reference | Homework | College | Grad | eLearning | Parents | Shop | Help

Search Encarta.com

Go   Reference   Encarta

Go to the World War II article.

Next

Albert Kesselring

Previous

View all pictures and sounds for World War II.

German field marshal Albert Kesselring, one of Adolf Hitler's top defense advisers in World War II (1939-1945), led the German air force during the Battle of Britain in 1940 and 1941.

Internet

▲ Field Marshal Albert Kesselring led the German air force during the Battle of Britain.

principal ally, attacked France from the south on June 10, 1940. By this time France was doomed. French leaders formally surrendered on June 22.

Great Britain now stood alone in Europe against the Germans. From September 1940 through May 1941, German aircraft bombed British cities practically every night. At sea the British navy fought German submarines that preyed on their merchant ships. Although facing overwhelming forces, the British suffered and fought through this period called the Battle of Britain. Prime Minister Winston Churchill said of his people, ". . . if the British Empire and its commonwealth last for a thousand years, men will say, 'This was their finest hour.'"[3]

On June 22, 1941, Hitler took his biggest gamble and attacked the Soviet Union. Over a 2,000-mile front, a 3-million-man German army stormed into Russia. At first, the assault pressed forward with ruthless efficiency. Armored columns advanced forty and fifty miles a day. Russia is a huge country and winter arrives there early. By December, fierce winds howled and the Russian wheat fields were covered with snow. Almost at the gates of Moscow, the German army was stopped. It marked the first time Hitler's mighty fighting machine tasted defeat.

▶ America Joins the War

While battles raged in Europe, the American people engaged in a war of words. The country was divided into two groups. One group was called the isolationists, and believed America should stay out of the war in Europe. The second group, the interventionists, felt that the United States should become involved at least to the extent of granting aid to Great Britain. President Franklin Roosevelt sided with the interventionists. Under the

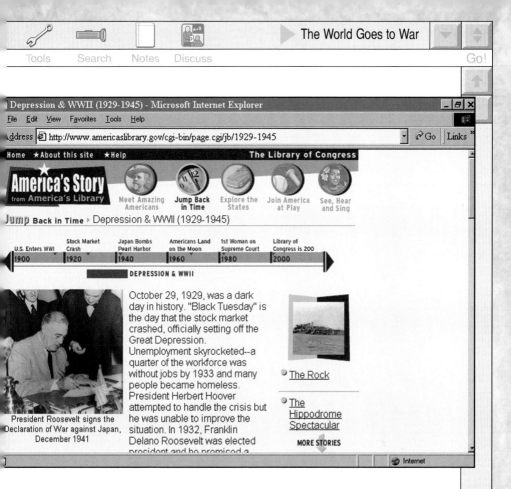

▲ President Franklin D. Roosevelt signed a declaration of war against Japan on December 8, 1941.

president's direction, the United States sent arms and food to the struggling people of England.

The American war of words ended on December 7, 1941. The day began as a routine Sunday at Pearl Harbor, Hawaii, in the Pacific Ocean. Shortly after dawn, Japanese planes roared over the American Pacific fleet. In a stunning battle that lasted less than two hours, the U.S. Navy lost eight battleships, and some 2,000 Americans were killed. The next day, President Roosevelt addressed Congress. He called December 7, "a date which will live in infamy." The president asked for and received a declaration of war against Japan.

Germany was loosely allied with Japan, but no treaty obliged Germany to enter this fight against the United States. Yet, on December 11, Adolf Hitler declared war on the United States. Italy soon followed with its own declaration. Historians still debate why the German leader waged war against the powerful nation across the Atlantic.

After Pearl Harbor, some fifty nations and more than half the world's population were involved in World War II. The combatants divided into two camps: the Axis and the Allies. The Axis consisted of Germany, Italy, and Japan. The Allies were made up of the United States, Great Britain (and its commonwealth partners including Canada, Australia, and New Zealand), and the Soviet Union. Germany and Italy were the major Axis participants in Europe.

Gearing for War, 1942

In the 1930s, the United States supported a tiny army. Smaller nations such as Portugal and Argentina had more soldiers than America did. Then came the attack on Pearl Harbor. Over the next three years, the services grew from about 400,000 members to a huge force of 16 million men and women. While millions volunteered for the army, navy, or marines, other young men simply waited to be

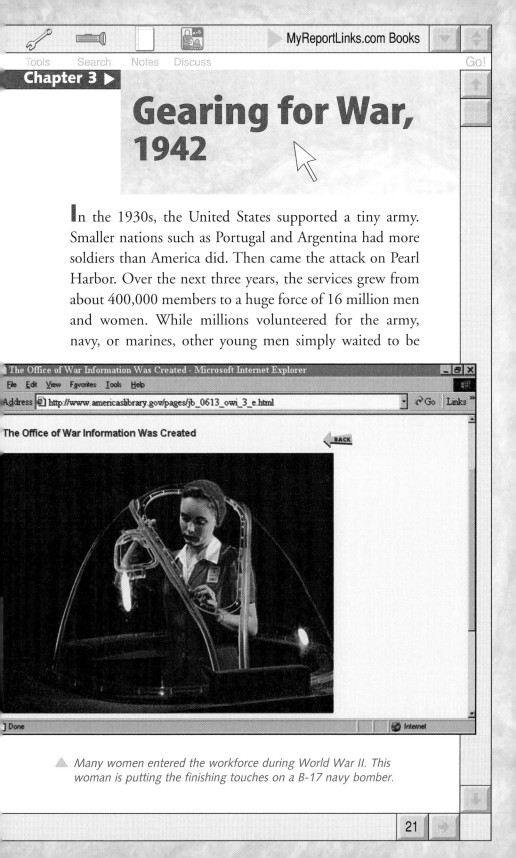

The Office of War Information Was Created - Microsoft Internet Explorer

File   Edit   View   Favorites   Tools   Help

Address   http://www.americaslibrary.gov/pages/jb_0613_owi_3_e.html   Go   Links

The Office of War Information Was Created

◀ BACK

▲ *Many women entered the workforce during World War II. This woman is putting the finishing touches on a B-17 navy bomber.*

called up or "drafted." All men aged eighteen through forty-five were required to register for the draft. Those drafted received a letter that began with the word "Greetings." Only a small number resisted the draft because most Americans considered World War II a "just war." Throughout history, governments, religious leaders, and individuals have wrestled with the idea of a just war, meaning a war that is moral and legal.

Equipping the newly formed army was a task for American industry. The United States had long had the most productive economy on Earth. However, the Great Depression of the 1930s closed factories and forced as many as one in four employees out of work. World War II brought the nation's huge factory network back to life. At breakneck speed, plants shifted from producing consumer goods to churning out weapons for war. For example, a company that once made typewriters now assembled machine guns. A manufacturer of pots and pans switched to turning out helmets for infantrymen.

Workers who suffered job losses during the Depression years found the factories begging for help. With millions of men in the armed forces, women were pressed into industrial work. In years past, women were thought to lack mechanical skills and were denied work in industrial plants. During the war, many factories had a workforce that was more than 50 percent female. African Americans usually faced discrimination when applying for industrial jobs. Wartime gave them new opportunities in industrial America.

With factories humming day and night, the country produced a staggering amount of military goods. The rugged army car—the jeep—jumped off assembly lines at the rate of one per minute. Almost 2.5 million trucks were produced in America during the war. When Germany

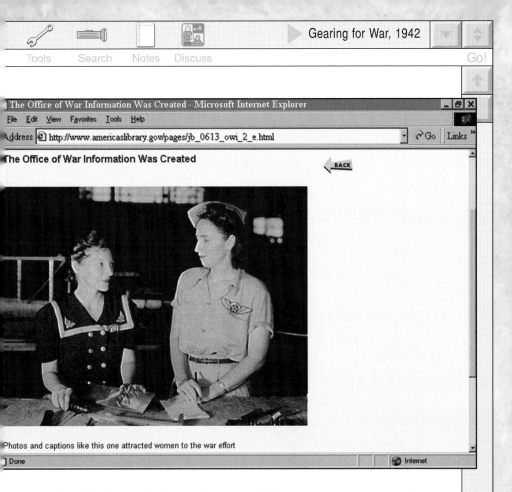

The Office of War Information Was Created - Microsoft Internet Explorer

File Edit View Favorites Tools Help

Address http://www.americaslibrary.gov/pages/jb_0613_owi_2_e.html Go Links

The Office of War Information Was Created

BACK

Photos and captions like this one attracted women to the war effort

Done Internet

With thousands of American men off at war, women were urged to work in industrial plants to support the war effort.

rumbled into Russia in 1940, it had 2,500 tanks, then the world's largest tank army. By the time the war ended, the United States Army was equipped with more than 100,000 tanks and self-propelled guns.

No American industry performed miracles on the scale of its shipyards. Many historians today reason that Adolf Hitler went to war with the United States because he believed the country could not build sufficient ships to make a difference in Europe. Never was the Führer more wrong. The United States produced the greatest collection of vessels the world had ever seen—with the aid of women

workers. Over the course of the conflict, shipyards in the United States assembled 5,425 large cargo ships and a gigantic fleet of warships.

Inside Nazi Germany

Germany's defeat in World War I brought humiliation and turmoil to the nation. Adolf Hitler promised to build a new nation that would forever heal the sting of defeat. In the 1930s, Hitler delivered on his promise. The Nazi government put people back to work. The trains ran on time. Soon the nation became a police state ruled by an ironhanded government, but at first no one seemed to notice.

Control of the school system was one of the first steps taken by the Nazis. Textbooks were rewritten and courses such as "racial science" introduced. Children were taught that blond, blue-eyed, "Aryan" people were superior to all others. Beyond the classroom, young Germans were compelled to join an organization called the Hitler Youth. Similar to the Boy Scouts, Hitler Youth members engaged in hiking, camping, and singing songs. Nazi propaganda permeated theses activities. At age ten, members were required to take an oath: "I swear to devote all my energies and my strength to the savior of our country, Adolf Hitler. I am willing and ready to give up my life for him, so help me God."[1]

After the conflict began, any German who questioned war aims was subject to arrest for treason. Those who belonged to political parties other than the Nazis were held in suspicion. People simply disappeared from their neighborhoods and towns. Whispered words said they were taken to barbed wire enclosed compounds in the countryside that were loosely called concentration camps.

Tools   Search   Notes   Discuss   Go!

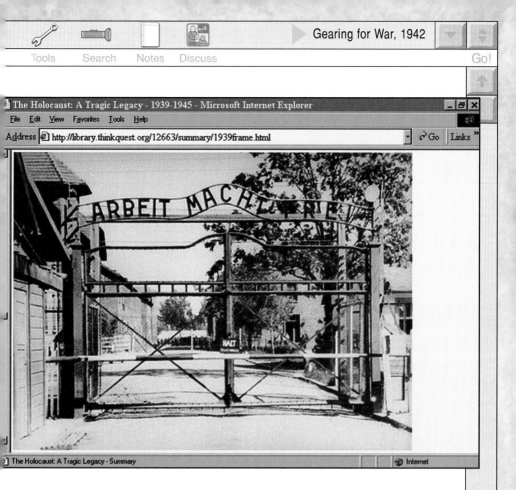

The Holocaust: A Tragic Legacy - 1939-1945 - Microsoft Internet Explorer

File Edit View Favorites Tools Help

Address http://library.thinkquest.org/12663/summary/1939frame.html   Go   Links

The Holocaust: A Tragic Legacy - Summary   Internet

▲ The entrance to Auschwitz. The Nazis murdered approximately 1.5 to 2 million people in this concentration camp. Ironically, the words inscribed on the gate "arbeit macht frie" translate to "work brings freedom."

Anyone who differed from the norm might be taken: Communists, homosexuals, the mentally and physically ill, and especially Jews.

After Germany occupied much of Europe, the Nazis began a reign of terror aimed at Jewish people. Death camps sprang up, especially in Eastern Europe. Today, just the names of those camps are horrible reminders of the Holocaust—Auschwitz, Buchenwald, Dachau, Treblinka. At the beginning of the war, the Jewish population of Europe numbered about 11 million. By war's end, some 6 million Jews had been put to death by the Nazis.

The Holocaust was an attempt at genocide; the attempt to slowly kill off a racial group. It seems incredible that a sophisticated country such as Germany could commit such horrific acts.

Strategy and Tactics

Weeks after the United States joined the war, President Roosevelt met with British Prime Minister Winston Churchill. The two Allied leaders agreed that the United States should concentrate on defeating Germany before focusing on Japan. Therefore, more American ships, tanks, and aircraft were sent to the European front than to the Pacific front. Although united on the "Europe First" policy, there were strong disagreements between the United States and Great Britain.

American military leaders George Marshall and Dwight Eisenhower wanted to build up forces on the British Isles and then launch a massive invasion of German-occupied France. The British argued that the German army was too strong in France, and therefore any invasion across the English Channel was doomed to fail. The British favored an assault on German territory by way of the Mediterranean Sea. This would mean a campaign advancing through Sicily, Italy, and then into the heart of Europe.

British will prevailed. The British assured United States leaders that the Mediterranean route would be an easier and wiser road. In several letters, Prime Minister Churchill referred to the Mediterranean and Italy as Europe's "soft underbelly."

Chapter 4

Taking the Offensive, 1943

Throughout the war years, far more German troops were engaged in fighting the Russians than in fighting the British and the Americans. In the fall of 1942, the mighty German army was once more rolling forward on the Russian front. To many observers—including large numbers of Russian officers—the German *Wehrmacht* (armed forces) seemed invincible.

▶ Agony at Stalingrad

The prime goal of the German thrust in southern Russia was the city of Stalingrad. Situated on the Volga River, the city was named after Joseph Stalin. It therefore had both military and political importance. In August 1942, German bombers roared over the city, reducing it to rubble. Then a German force of 300,000 men—the flower of the Wehrmacht—attacked. Russian soldiers burrowed into the wreckage and refused to be

The Eastern Front

→ → → ▶
The German Advance

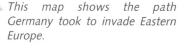

▲ This map shows the path Germany took to invade Eastern Europe.

flushed out. Fighting was relentless, house-to-house and street-to-street. German soldiers called it *Rattenkrieg* (War of the Rats).

Winter came, burying the ruined city in snow. Still, the opposing soldiers fought with rifles, hand grenades, and often with knives and bare hands. In late November, Russian tank units situated outside the city attacked the Germans from the north and south and encircled the German troops. Temperatures dropped to –40°F. Ammunition and food supplies dwindled. A trapped

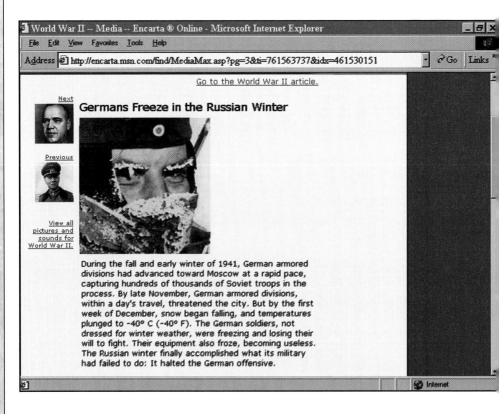

World War II -- Media -- Encarta ® Online - Microsoft Internet Explorer

File Edit View Favorites Tools Help

Address http://encarta.msn.com/find/MediaMax.asp?pg=3&ti=761563737&idx=461530151 | Go | Links

Go to the World War II article.

Next

Previous

View all pictures and sounds for World War II.

Germans Freeze in the Russian Winter

During the fall and early winter of 1941, German armored divisions had advanced toward Moscow at a rapid pace, capturing hundreds of thousands of Soviet troops in the process. By late November, German armored divisions, within a day's travel, threatened the city. But by the first week of December, snow began falling, and temperatures plunged to -40° C (-40° F). The German soldiers, not dressed for winter weather, were freezing and losing their will to fight. Their equipment also froze, becoming useless. The Russian winter finally accomplished what its military had failed to do: It halted the German offensive.

Internet

Perhaps one of Hitler's biggest mistakes was his attempt to capture Stalingrad. Unprepared for the harsh weather, many German soldiers froze to death during the winter of 1942–43.

German officer wrote his wife, "Around me everything is collapsing, a whole army is dying . . ."[1]

German Field Marshal Friedrich von Paulus surrendered his Sixth Army on January 31, 1943. The final blow came on February 2, when the rest of the German forces at Stalingrad surrendered. More than 300,000 German soldiers were lost at Stalingrad. The myth of Wehrmacht invincibility died there as well. After the winter of 1942–43, the Germans never again launched a successful sustained offensive against the Russians.

Desert Defeat

Staff Sergeant William Thornton, U.S. Army, wrote this entry in his diary shortly after his unit fought a major battle against the Germans in North Africa. "Corporal Clifford missing in action. Morale quite low. Corporal Apuntius and Private Cardorick breaking down from nervous strain due to shell shock."[2]

A freezing morning greeted American soldiers protecting a gap in the mountains called the Kasserine Pass. It was February 1943 in the bleak desert country of the North African continent. Suddenly the defenders were struck by a hurricane of artillery fire. Rockets from six-barreled launchers streaked the sky and crashed into American positions. For the first time since landing in North Africa, American soldiers were subjected to a frightening artillery barrage. It would not be the last.

When the artillery fire lifted, enemy infantry supported by waves of tanks advanced on the American front. Many American units fought a gallant but disorganized battle. Hundreds of young soldiers panicked and ran. A sergeant later wrote, "The road [to Kasserine Pass] was a chaos of retreating Americans and their transport."[3]

▲ *The Tuskegee Airmen were the first African-American pilots in the U.S. military. They contributed to American military operations in Europe and North Africa. Pictured here are Col. Benjamin O. Davis (right) and Lieutenant Lee Rayford.*

The Battle of Kasserine Pass was a bitter defeat. In two days the American army lost 300 dead and 3,000 wounded, and a shocking number—almost 3,000—surrendered to the enemy. The American chief, General Dwight D. Eisenhower, blamed the loss at Kasserine on, "greenness, particularly among commanders."[4]

▶ Sicily, First Step in the Mediterranean

In May 1943, North Africa fell to forces of the United States and Great Britain. Hitler's heralded *Afrika Korps*, led by the dynamic general Erwin Rommel, had been overrun. Some 350,000 Axis soldiers were killed, wounded, or captured during the North African campaign. The Allies next set their sights on the Mediterranean island of Sicily.

Code-named "Husky," the invasion of Sicily began on July 10, 1943. At dawn, thousands of American and British troops splashed out of landing craft and made their way inland. The Germans fought a defensive campaign, digging into Sicily's steep hillsides and stone farmhouses. Advancing against these strongholds was a perilous task. Whenever possible the Americans pounded German positions with heavy artillery and bombs from airplanes first. Grudgingly, the Germans grew to respect the fighting abilities of United States soldiers. A letter found on the body of a German infantryman said, "These astonishing

http://webpub.alleg.edu/student/p/paynes/images/europe/infantry/sicily.jpg - Microsoft Internet Explorer

File   Edit   View   Favorites   Tools   Help

Address http://webpub.alleg.edu/student/p/paynes/images/europe/infantry/sicily.jpg   Go   Links »

Done   Internet

▲ Allied soldiers invaded Sicily on July 10, 1943.

Americans. They fight all day, attack all night and shoot all the time."[5]

The Allies captured Sicily in a thirty-eight day campaign. Taking the island cost United States forces about 7,500 men killed or wounded. In one respect, the conquest was a disappointment. The Americans had hoped to isolate thousands of German defenders on the island and take them prisoner. However, the bulk of German troops crossed the Strait of Messina and escaped to Italy.

▶ Fortress Italy

The hearts and energies of the average Italian were never devoted to this war. During the fighting over Sicily, Italians demanded the removal of their leader—the dictator Benito Mussolini. When Mussolini was thrown out of office in July 1943, Italian forces were essentially taken out of World War II. Americans hoped the change in government would ease the conquest of Italy. Hours after Mussolini's collapse, however, Hitler ordered the thousands of German troops already in Italy to take command of the peninsula.

On September 9, 1943, a fleet of 500 Allied ships approached the Italian port city of Salerno. It was a strangely silent night. Hoping to catch the Germans by surprise the warships did not fire their huge guns. Soldiers soon discovered the Germans were far from surprised. As the Americans climbed onto landing beaches, they were greeted by a German voice, speaking in English: "Give up, you have no chance." Minutes later, German defenders blasted the Americans with artillery and withering machine gun fire. Salerno was a bloody landing in what would prove to be a bloody Italian campaign.

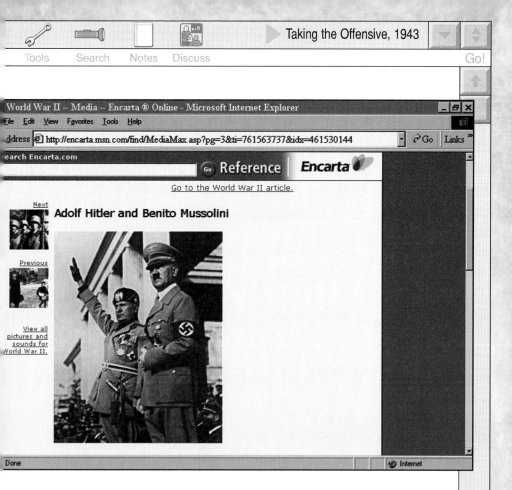

▲ *Benito Mussolini and Adolf Hitler, both Fascist dictators, were friends and allies. They are pictured here in Munich, Germany, in 1937. A few years later in 1943, Hitler sent thousands of German troops into Italy.*

Six days of heavy fighting were needed to secure the Salerno beachhead.

A cagey general named Albert Kesselring commanded German troops in Italy. American officers nicknamed Kesselring "Smiling Al," because he always seemed to be smiling in news films. He was a genius at letting the mountains and valleys of Italy work for him. Mountain ranges roll over Italy like waves at sea. Such terrain is a paradise for a defender and a nightmare for the attacker.

Kesselring laid out a series of defensive lines that gave his troops full advantage of the high ground. When well

dug in on a mountaintop, one hundred of his men could stop the advance of a thousand Allied soldiers. Kesselring allowed the Allies to advance yard by yard, paying for every yard of ground with blood. When the enemy was upon him, Kesselring simply pulled his men back to the next well-prepared defensive line. Smiling Al's tactics worked to perfection. Italy became an ordeal for the Allied armies.

Particularly frustrating was the German-held Gustav Line, which crossed Italy just above the port city of Naples. At the heart of this defensive line rose the 1,700-foot Monte Cassino. Time after time, the Allies assaulted the mountain only to be driven back at a terrible cost in lives.

The Americans tried to go around the Gustav Line by landing at the port city of Anzio on January 22, 1944. The landing failed to break the German grip on Italy, and Anzio became a killing ground.

It was not until June 1944 that the Americans marched into Rome. By that time Allied leaders realized they could not win the war in Europe with a thrust through Italy. Winston Churchill once had called Italy Europe's "soft underbelly." American General Mark Clark more accurately described the Italian peninsula as "a tough old gut."

Ernie Pyle, a widely read journalist who followed the American army through many battles in Italy, described what he saw: "Our troops were living in almost inconceivable misery. The fertile black valleys [of Italy] were knee deep in mud. Thousands of the men had not been dry for weeks."[6]

▶ The Air War

At the start of World War II, Herman Göring, the chief of the German Air Force, made a boast: "If bombs drop on

Germany, my name is Meyer." It was a sarcastic remark because Meyer is often a German-Jewish name. Then thousands of tons of bombs began falling on Germany, and by the end of 1942 angry crowds on city streets shouted at Göring, "Herr Meyer! Herr Meyer!"[7]

Throughout 1943, American and British bombers pounded German targets around the clock. The British preferred area bombing. British bombers swept over cities at night dropping thousands of incendiary bombs and leaving whole cities in flames. The Americans concentrated on daylight precision bombing. Flying four-engine B-17 and B-24 bombers, American crews destroyed bridges, railroads, and factory complexes.

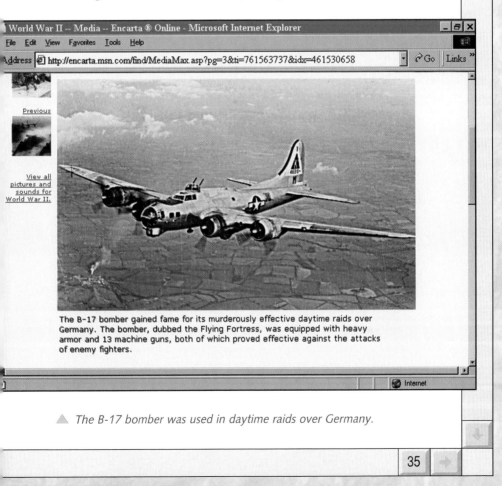

World War II -- Media -- Encarta ® Online - Microsoft Internet Explorer

File Edit View Favorites Tools Help

Address http://encarta.msn.com/find/MediaMax.asp?pg=3&ti=761563737&idx=461530658 Go Links

Previous

View all pictures and sounds for World War II.

The B-17 bomber gained fame for its murderously effective daytime raids over Germany. The bomber, dubbed the Flying Fortress, was equipped with heavy armor and 13 machine guns, both of which proved effective against the attacks of enemy fighters.

Internet

▲ The B-17 bomber was used in daytime raids over Germany.

In August 1943, a force of 376 American B-17s struck the German city of Schweinfurt where ball bearings were manufactured. The raid was a disaster for American bomber crews. Over Schweinfurt, sixty B-17s were shot down by German fighter planes and by antiaircraft fire. Schweinfurt and similar missions gave B-17 and B-24 flyers some of the highest casualty rates of all American services in World War II.

A "miracle" fighter plane came to the aid of the bombers in early 1944. The P-51 Mustang was a single-engine craft that could reach speeds of 450 mph. Best of all, it had extraordinary range. P-51s were able to take off with the bombers and make the 1,500-mile round trip to Germany from bases in England. The highly maneuverable Mustang fought off German planes as they attempted to shoot down the American bombers. Many aviation experts today conclude the American-built Mustang was the finest fighter plane of World War II.

With the Americans and British finally in control of the skies, terror and death became a grim reality for German city dwellers. In July 1943, hundreds of British and American bombers raided the industrial city of Hamburg. Incendiary bombs started a fire so huge it sucked in air from the countryside, creating winds strong enough to topple automobiles. At least fifty thousand men, women, and children were killed in the Hamburg bombings. A high Nazi official visiting Hamburg wrote, "A city of a million inhabitants has been destroyed in a manner unparalleled in history."[8]

Assault Through France, 1944

On a moonlit night, more than nine hundred twin-engine aircraft roared over the English Channel. The planes flew in tight formations, almost wingtip to wingtip. Inside sat more than 13,000 paratroopers, all of them nervously awaiting a signal to jump. Searchlight beams pierced the sky along the French coastline. Explosions from antiaircraft shells rocked the formations. Through portholes men saw planes bursting to pieces and twisting to the ground. Said one pilot, "It seemed almost impossible to fly through that wall of fire without getting shot down, but I had no choice. There was no turning back."[1]

▶ D-Day Is Launched

Over France the paratroopers jumped. In the confusion and the blackness of night, most landed near the wrong targets and were lost for hours. Many paratroopers fell into the middle of German troop concentrations and were killed before their feet touched French soil. It was these airborne soldiers who launched D-Day, the long-awaited assault on German-occupied France.

Bobbing in the waters off the French coast at Normandy were 9,000 vessels, large and small. It was the biggest fleet of ships ever assembled. Crammed in the vessels were 250,000 sailors and infantrymen. At dawn, the Allies' heavy-gunned warships opened fire on the waiting German troops. The coast at Normandy disappeared under a curtain of explosions. Troops assembled on the

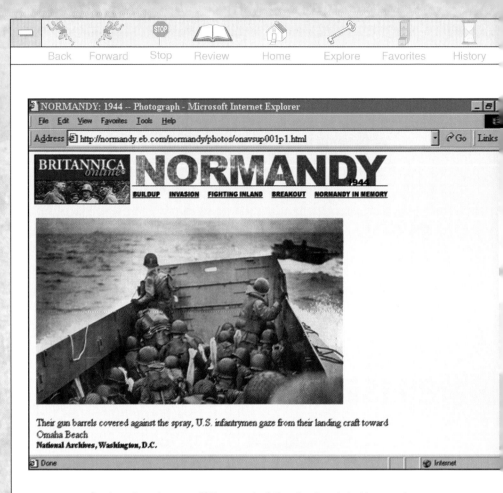

▲ American troops off the coast of Omaha Beach in Normandy.

decks gasped. No one, they believed, could live through a bombardment so powerful.

Landing craft, each crowded with fifty or more troops, churned toward beaches with code names—Omaha, Utah, Gold, Sword, Juno. An inferno greeted American soldiers hitting the beach at Omaha. Dozens of landing craft were blown apart in the water. Other boats butted against the beach, and dropped their ramps, only to have their passengers sprayed by German machine-gun fire. Private Harry Parley, an American soldier who landed at Omaha Beach on June 6, 1944, later recalled, "As our boat touched the sand and the ramp went down I became a visitor to hell."[2]

Somehow the men pushed forward on Omaha and the other beaches. By afternoon, ground units had moved inland far enough to link up with the airborne soldiers. In his book about D-Day, Stephen Ambrose wrote, "Nearly 175,000 American, Canadian, and British troops had entered Normandy, either by air or sea at a cost of 4,900 casualties."[3] He also noted, "No exact figures are possible either for the number of men landed or for casualties, for D-Day alone."[4]

Breakout in France

Prior to D-Day the Allies played a deadly cat-and-mouse game with the Germans. Both sides knew an invasion of France would take place. The question was where. German military leaders believed the invasion would come at the Pas-de-Calais. There the Channel is so narrow one can stand on English soil and see the coast of France on a clear day. The Allies chose Normandy largely because the Germans would not expect an assault in that region.

American and British officers expected to follow D-Day with a rapid sweep through France. This was not the case. The countryside in Normandy was laced with dirt and stone fences called hedgerows. German defenders were able to crouch behind these natural obstacles and fire on advancing troops. For six weeks, the Allies were stuck in hedgerow country. Finally, in mid-July, tanks and infantry broke out of Normandy.

Once on the French flatlands, the Allies staged a blitzkrieg of their own. Some units advanced thirty miles a day. Paris was liberated on August 25, 1944. The Nazis, it seemed, were doomed. General Eisenhower bet

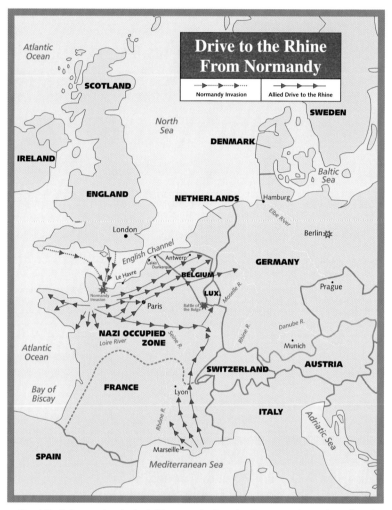

Drive to the Rhine From Normandy

- ▶ ▶ ▶ Normandy Invasion
- → → → Allied Drive to the Rhine

▲ Allied forces landed at Normandy Beach, France. They then fought their way to the Rhine River, and into Germany.

British General Montgomery five British pounds (then twenty-five dollars) that the war in Europe would be over by Christmas. This was followed by the Battle of the Bulge, which was a prelude to the final Allied victory in Europe.

Victory in Europe, 1945

Not since the time of Napoléon had an enemy army crossed the Rhine River and penetrated German soil. In February 1945, the German infantry fell behind this natural barrier and prepared for a last stand. Systematically the Germans blew up Rhine bridges to deny the Allies a river crossing. All bridges were destroyed except for one.

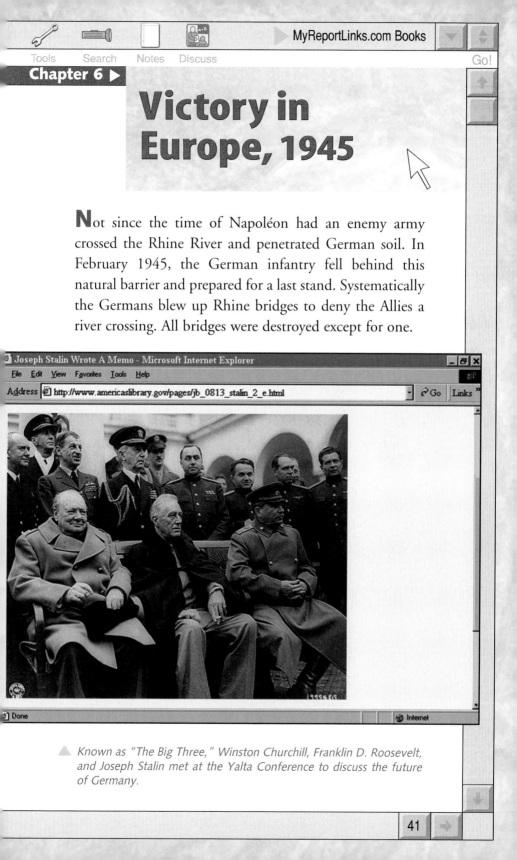

Joseph Stalin Wrote A Memo - Microsoft Internet Explorer

File   Edit   View   Favorites   Tools   Help

Address http://www.americaslibrary.gov/pages/jb_0813_stalin_2_e.html   Go   Links

Done   Internet

▲ *Known as "The Big Three," Winston Churchill, Franklin D. Roosevelt, and Joseph Stalin met at the Yalta Conference to discuss the future of Germany.*

On March 7, 1945, American tanks and infantry approached the city of Remagen. The Americans could scarcely believe what they saw ahead. There stood a steel bridge, perfectly intact, spanning the Rhine. At that moment, German engineers worked feverishly to wire explosives onto the bridge supports. The Americans rushed across before German engineers could complete their task. The capture of the bridge at Remagen was one of the great fortunes of World War II. Within twenty-four hours, more than 8,000 Americans were on the east side of the Rhine.

Far to the east, the Russian army rolled forward toward Berlin, Germany. On April 25, Russian and American patrols met at the town of Torgau, about 75 miles south of Berlin. Russians and Americans danced and sang together despite the fact they could not speak each other's language. War-weary soldiers on both sides knew this fight would soon be over.

There was, however, one tremendous battle left to be fought. In early April, a Russian army of 4 million men approached Berlin. The most devastating fighting in Europe had taken place between Germany and Russia. Russian soldiers killed eight out of every ten German troops killed in the field. Still, Russian losses totaled an incredible 25 million soldiers and civilians during the course of the war.

The Battle of Berlin was the final tragedy in the bloody clash between Germany and Russia. The Germans sent Hitler Youth boys as young as twelve into the streets to fight Russian tanks. Berliners huddled in cellars while their city was pounded by Russian artillery. Hardly a building was left standing in the German capital. An estimated 100,000 German troops and an equal number of Russians were killed in the fight over this last Nazi stronghold.

Hitler and his close advisers occupied a bunker deep underground in the center of Berlin. On April 30, Russian soldiers were so close to the bunker that guards outside could hear their rifle fire. In a bizarre ceremony, Hitler married his girlfriend of many years, Eva Braun. Shortly after the ceremony, Eva took poison and died. At 3:15 P.M., Adolf Hitler, who dreamed of building an empire, bit down on a poison capsule while at the same time firing a pistol bullet into his head.[1] German guards burned their bodies.

On May 7, 1945, German General Alfred Jodl signed the Allied surrender terms. The European war had lasted

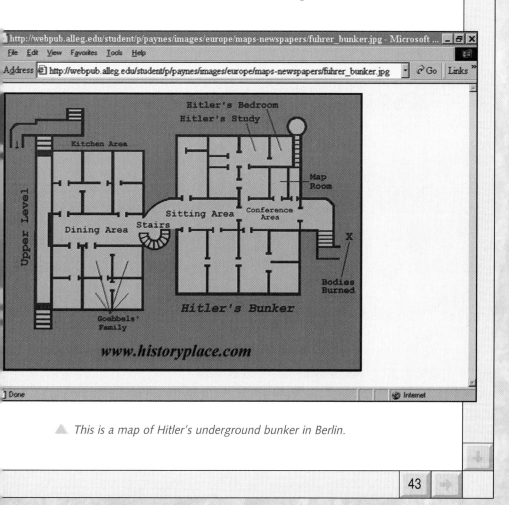

This is a map of Hitler's underground bunker in Berlin.

five years, eight months, and seven days. General Eisenhower had lost his bet with Montgomery, but the war in Europe was finally over.

General George C. Marshall sent the following message to General Dwight D. Eisenhower. "You have completed your mission with the greatest victory in the history of warfare."[2]

▷ Aftermath

The war left most of Europe in shambles. Millions of people had little food and inadequate or no housing. Worst of all, the end of the European conflict brought

http://gi.grolier.com/wwii/photos/USWW004&.JPEG - Microsoft Internet Explorer

File   Edit   View   Favorites   Tools   Help

Address http://gi.grolier.com/wwii/photos/USWW004&.JPEG   Go   Links

Done   Internet

▲ Crowds gathered in New York City's Times Square to celebrate the end of the war in Europe.

international tensions instead of lasting peace. The Communist Soviet Union was now the dominant power on the European continent. Soviet armies occupied Poland, East Germany, Hungary, Czechoslovakia, and other eastern European regions. It seemed likely the Soviet leaders would install Communist governments in those eastern countries regardless of the wishes of their people. The Russians and the Americans—once allies—became bitter enemies in a new test of wills called the Cold War.

The end of the European war did not end World War II. The end finally came after the United States dropped two atomic bombs on Japan, and when on September 2, 1945, representatives of Japan officially surrendered aboard the battleship USS *Missouri*. Yet the conclusion of the European war sparked celebrations. Paris church bells rang. Crowds gathered in front of Buckingham Palace in London and sang "God Save the King." People crowded into New York's Times Square to shout and laugh. World War II in Europe was over at last.

Chapter 1. The Battle of the Bulge
1. Allan R. Millett and Peter Maslowski, *For the Common Defense: A Military History of the United States of America* (New York: The Free Press, 1994), p. 480.

Chapter 2. The World Goes to War
1. William L. Shirer, *The Rise and Fall of the Third Reich* (New York: Simon & Schuster, 1960), p. 599.

2. Robert Edwin Herzstein, *The Nazis* (Alexandria, Va.: Time-Life Books, 1980), p. 124.

3. Winston S. Churchill, *Their Finest Hour* (Boston: Houghton Mifflin, 1948), p. 226.

Chapter 3. Gearing for War, 1942
1. William L. Shirer, *The Rise and Fall of the Third Reich* (New York: Simon & Schuster, 1960), p. 253.

Chapter 4. Taking the Offensive, 1943
1. C. L. Sulzberger, *The American Heritage History of World War II* (New York: American Heritage Books, 1966), p. 298.

2. Edwin P. Hoyt, *The GI's War* (New York: McGraw-Hill, 1988), p. 176.

3. Charles Whiting, *Kasserine: First Blood* (New York: Stein and Day, 1984), p. 206.

4. Dwight D. Eisenhower, *Crusade in Europe* (New York: Doubleday & Co., 1948), p. 147.

5. Robert Wallace, *The Italian Campaign* (Alexandria, Va.: Time-Life Books, 1978), p. 31.

6. Sulzberger, p. 386.

7. Ibid., p. 417.

8. William L. Shirer, *The Rise and Fall of the Third Reich* (New York: Simon & Schuster, 1960), p. 1,009.

Chapter 5. Assault Through France, 1944
1. Stephen E. Ambrose, *D-Day June 6, 1941: The Climatic Battle of World War II* (New York: Simon & Schuster, 1994), p. 335.

2. Ibid., p. 199.

3. Ibid., p. 576.

4. Ibid.

Chapter 6. Victory in Europe, 1945
1. John Toland, *Adolf Hitler*, vol. II (New York: Doubleday, 1976), p. 1,002.

2. Stephen E. Ambrose, *The Victors* (New York: Simon & Schuster, 1998), p. 346.

Further Reading

Ambrose, Stephen E. *D-Day June 6, 1941: The Climatic Battle of World War II.* New York: Simon & Schuster, 1994.

————. *The Victors.* New York: Simon & Schuster, 1998.

Anderson, Carla. *World War II.* New York: Penguin Putnam Books for Young Readers, 1999.

Churchill, Winston S. *Their Finest Hour.* Boston: Houghton Mifflin, 1948.

Eisenhower, Dwight D. *Crusade in Europe.* New York: Doubleday & Co, 1948.

Gay, Kathlyn and Martin K. Gay. *World War II.* Brookfield, Conn.: Twenty-First Century Books, Inc., 1995.

Herzstein, Robert Edwin. *The Nazis.* Alexandria, Va.: Time-Life Books, 1980.

Hoyt, Edwin P. *The GI's War.* New York: McGraw-Hill, 1988.

Landau, Elaine. *Nazi War Criminals.* Danbury, Conn.: Franklin Watts, 1990.

Reynoldson, Floria. *Women & War.* Austin, Tex.: Raintree Steck-Vaughn Publishers, 1993.

Saldinger, Anne Grenn. *Life in a Nazi Concentration Camp.* Farmington Hills, Mich.: Gale Group, 2000.

Shirer, William L. *The Rise and Fall of the Third Reich.* New York: Simon & Schuster, 1960.

Stein, R. Conrad. *World War II in Europe: "America Goes to War."* Hillside, N.J.: Enslow Publishers, Inc., 1994.